T0386272

ANDY'S GONE

ANDY'S GONE

MARIE-CLAUDE VERDIER
TRANSLATED BY ALEXIS DIAMOND

PLAYWRIGHTS CANADA PRESS
TORONTO

For professional or amateur production rights, please contact:
Karine Lapierre, Agence RBL
118-410 Saint-Nicolas, Montreal, Quebec H2Y 2P5
514.564.5644 ext. 107 | karine@agencerbl.com

LIBRARY AND ARCHIVES CANADA CATALOGUING IN PUBLICATION
Title: Andy's gone / Marie-Claude Verdier ; translated by Alexis Diamond.
Other titles: Andy's gone. English | Andy is gone
Names: Verdier, Marie-Claude, author. | Diamond, Alexis (Playwright), translator. | Adaptation of (Work) Sophocles. Antigone.
Description: A play. | Translation of: Andy's gone. | Adaption of: Antigone.
Identifiers: Canadiana (print) 20210139048 | Canadiana (ebook) 20210139315 | ISBN 9780369102188 (softcover) | ISBN 9780369102195 (PDF) | ISBN 9780369102201 (HTML) | ISBN 9780369102218 (Kindle)
Classification: LCC PS8643.E7155 A713 2021 | DDC C842/.92—dc23

Playwrights Canada Press operates on Mississaugas of the Credit, Wendat, Anishinaabe, Métis, and Haudenosaunee land. It always was and always will be Indigenous land.

We acknowledge the financial support of the Government of Canada through the National Translation Program for Book Publishing, an initiative of the *Roadmap for Canada's Official Languages 2013-2019: Education, Immigration, Communities*, for our translation activities. We acknowledge the financial support of the Canada Council for the Arts, the Ontario Arts Council (OAC), Ontario Creates, and the Government of Canada for our publishing activities.

Canada Council for the Arts Conseil des arts du Canada

ONTARIO ARTS COUNCIL
CONSEIL DES ARTS DE L'ONTARIO
an Ontario government agency
un organisme du gouvernement de l'Ontario

Canadä

ONTARIO CREATES | ONTARIO CRÉATIF

To Julien

—MCV

AUTHOR'S NOTE

When director Julien Bouffier approached me to adapt Jean Anouilh's *Antigone*, I must admit I felt a bit overwhelmed. Would I be able to find a way to create my own rendition of this work, so often adapted for theatre and television, that would still feel relevant today? But Julien already had very specific parameters in mind. The play would be aimed at high-school audiences, and performed in all kinds of settings, but mostly in classrooms. And it would be the soundtrack, broadcast through headsets worn by audience members, that would establish the world of the characters. A heady challenge for a playwright.

This initial meeting launched a productive and sustained conversation, right up to the opening performance. Julien quickly decided that our story would focus on the conflict between Creon and Antigone, and that Creon would be a woman. Two women facing off over the future of the city. Two women who could be sisters, each a reflection of the other through the mirror of time. We then realized that Antigone's act of defiance couldn't remain private, that it had to be public and altruistic. It was important for me to address the theme of altruism with this audience. To show that it is possible for each one of us to make our mark on the world, even if we are young and feel very much left out of the decisions made on a global scale. The writing took off in this direction, and

I was able to finish the play on the other side of the Atlantic, in the final rehearsals.

To date, the show has been performed more than a hundred times, and I never cease to be amazed by the audience members' reaction—both the young and the not-so-young—to this encounter with theatre, the unconventional form allowing it to be presented in classrooms, often to students who have never before seen live theatre. I am delighted that this play could make the journey into English to encounter new audiences. It is a joy to be joined in this endeavour by Alexis Diamond, whose sharp intelligence and humour make it possible for the words to retain their power and nuance in translation.

TRANSLATOR'S NOTE

Marie-Claude Verdier and I first met at a translation conference held by the Centre des auteurs/autrices dramatiques (CEAD) in Montreal in the summer of 2012. In one of the assigned exercises, we were instructed to render a piece of dialogue from a well-known text into a certain style. I opted for *Hamlet* as a 1950s film noir, with a bit of help from the wonderful theatre artist and translator Leanna Brodie. Then we presented our bits of translation folly to the group. My slip of text got some laughs. And Marie-Claude, who was then a dramaturg at CEAD, came over to (re)introduce herself and tell me she really liked my bit. Then we all went home.

Shortly thereafter, Playwrights' Workshop Montréal (PWM) announced that they were launching an award to promote theatre translation of Québécois plays into English by training emerging translators. Marie-Claude contacted me about submitting her play *Je n'y suis plus*. I read it and fell in love. We submitted the work for translation, and in 2013 we were awarded the inaugural PWM Cole Foundation Mentorship for Emerging Translators with the inimitable Maureen Labonté. And thus was launched an enduring friendship as well as a lifelong collaboration.

To my mind, the translation of a work of art is one of the most intimate relationships there can be. It means entering the author's mind, imagination, their way of seeing things.

To do Marie-Claude justice, I had to understand the world she created through language, inside and out. And each time I approach a new text of Marie-Claude's, I delve further into her theatre universe, which is vast, epically complex and achingly human.

To render her text justice, I had to reach beyond Marie-Claude's direct inspiration, Anouilh's *Antigone*, to Sophocles's original, which only compounded the challenges involved in translating this text: it is a contemporary text that draws on a classical one; it is a highly theatrical poetic text intended for performance in everyday school settings; it is structured so that it alternates between public proclamations addressed directly to the audience and private tête-à-têtes overheard through headsets. The constant tension is wrought between the archaic and the current, the public and the private, the poetic and the quasi-mundane. The English translation is the result of this impossible but worthy and wholly pleasurable quest to find a balance between the text's concision and richness, its politics and poetry.

Andy's Gone was first produced in French by Adesso e Sempre in 2016. There were three public readings: the first was supported by Le Conseil départemental de l'Hérault, after a week-long residence in Béziers; the second at Le Printemps des comédiens, Montpellier, from June 24 to 26; and the third at Le Tarmac, Scène internationale francophone, Paris, from June 27 to 29. The first performance was at Collège Lucie Aubrac, Béziers, on November 14. The play featured the following cast and creative team:

Vanessa Liautey
Zoé Martelli

Director: Julien Bouffier
Sound Design: Jean-Christophe Sirven

CHARACTERS

Alison
Regina

The Absent:
Andy/Henry
The Units

1. ASSEMBLY

Community hall.

Chairs scattered throughout the space.
Curtains are drawn over the windows.
The room is dark.
On the wall, three neon tubes make an H.

REGINA, *elegant and understated, in a black and purple suit,*
Bluetooth device in her ear, sits facing the H.

When we enter, the technician hands us a headset and motions
for us to take a seat.

REGINA *(voice-over in our headsets)*
Welcome. You are safe here. Thank you for coming so
quickly after I called the curfew. Your compliance and com-
posure do you credit. Here we have everything we need,
and here we will remain, together, until order has been
restored outside. I commend you all for your civic-mind-
edness. It is due to citizens such as yourselves that the city
will endure. I am glad I am able to count on you. A queen
must be able to count on her subjects. In difficult moments
such as these, we must stay united.

REGINA gets up and stands next to the luminous H. She addresses us directly.

There are words we do not want to utter.
Words that swell in the throat.
Words made of bristles and barbs
Thistles and thorns
Wails and woe
Words that crack the heart
Hone the hurt
I never knew these words
A foreign tongue.
Unknown horror.
But I must
I am announcing
I
Excuse me.
Prince Henry died this morning.
And the sky came undone.
As though it sensed my loss.
Our pain.
I had to shut the gates.
We had just enough time to bury him.
At the cemetery, a lone flag stands watch.
But, now that we are all safe.
I would like us to take this moment.
To remember him.
That proud, brave boy. An example. Our example.
We will now observe a moment of silence to honour his memory.

REGINA remains standing.
She receives a call on her Bluetooth device.
Annoyed, she glares at the technician.
The volume of the music in the headsets goes up.

(into the Bluetooth device) I'm here. The curfew will stay in effect as long as the threat remains. Forget the meteorologists' predictions: your units will maintain their positions and patrol the walls for as long as I say. No one must walk along the walls, under pain of death. Shoot to kill. No exceptions. Is that clear? No. I went to her room this morning and she wasn't there. I don't know. You need to find her. Everything's changed. Keep me in the loop.

REGINA returns to her spot at the front, where she continues to pull herself together.

Suddenly the music in the headsets is interrupted.
Sounds of interference. In the headsets we hear police chatter.

UNIT 8
This is Unit 8, we are in position near the east wall with Unit 5. Nothing to report.

UNIT 3
Copy that, Unit 8. Stay sharp. I will continue to patrol the cemetery.

UNIT 5
What are the weather predictions? The storm is supposed to hit when, exactly?

UNIT 8
What's that noise outside the walls?

UNIT 3
Unit 8, do not approach the parapet!

UNIT 8
I think it's . . . voices. Do you hear that?

UNIT 5
What are you talking about?

UNIT 8
I'm telling you . . .

UNIT 3
Shit!

UNIT 5
Situation report, Unit 3?

UNIT 3
Someone took the flag from Prince Henry's grave!

UNIT 5
Terrific. And where were you?

UNIT 3
I can't be everywhere at once!

UNIT 8
Someone just went through the parking lot.

UNIT 5
In pursuit.

UNIT 3
With you.

REGINA feels faint. She sits back down. The technician gives her a bottle of water and returns to their station.

UNIT 8
Eyes on. Hey, it's a girl!

UNIT 5
We've been made!

UNIT 3
Do not approach!

UNIT 8
Shit! She's lit the flag on fire!

UNIT 5
There's smoke everywhere. I can't see a thing. We need to put that out before it reaches the vehicles.

UNIT 8
Stop! Police! Drop the flag!

UNIT 5
Requesting backup.

UNIT 8
She took off, quick as a cat.

UNIT 3
Where'd she go?

UNIT 8
She left a tag on the wall, a funny-looking A with an arrow.

UNIT 5
Fire under control. Pursuing suspect.

UNIT 3
Attention, all units. Critical situation at the north gate. All units, report immediately.

UNIT 5
Christ! We can't let her get away!

UNIT 8
Don't you think she looks like . . .

UNIT 3
Critical means now. We'll find her later; she's the only one out on the streets.

UNIT 5
Roger that. On our way.

2. THE CITY

REGINA stands. She signals to the technician and the music in the headsets ceases.

REGINA
Thank you for your attention.
This is a difficult time.
But have no fear.
All will be well.
I will do everything in my power to ensure nothing changes.
Our city has been here for generations.
Our lands are fertile.
Our forests have been rising for centuries.
We have been here as long as they.
We have watched ourselves grow.
Our roots are interlaced.
We belong to each other.
Our valley is lovely.
Earning their envy.
As though we were not worthy.
As though it has all been so easy.
But we work hard in the fields.
In our businesses.
In our schools and our hospitals.

None of this has been simple.
Our ancestors knew it.
Every generation has faced a usurper.
If not the Romans
Then the Cathars or the Saracens.
The Germans or the Italians.
We have always had to defend what is ours.
Even the elements, like today
Rise against us.
And when people defend themselves, they raise their
shields.
They build walls.
To protect themselves.
We must build them higher.
Still.
Look
Look at our city.
Look at our engineering, our sculptures, our parks
Our civilization.
Everything we have accomplished over generations.
And what will be handed down to Henry.
Our future.

Beat.
She pulls herself together.

Excuse me.
The world will no longer be his.
The world I prepared.
Protected.
Carefully guarded.

Excuse me.

Everything will go to my brother's daughter.

The next in line.

Alison.

But never fear. I will not be stepping down right away.

I still have plenty of good years in me.

To protect you.

I also have great plans for us.

We must add a metre to the east wing, and reinforce the gate . . .

REGINA gets a call. The technician signals to her. She ignores them. ALISON's voice infiltrates the headsets while REGINA speaks.

ALISON *(in the headsets)*	REGINA
Who's this woman speaking to you?	Since my coronation, I have had my heart set
The one standing there.	On this plan,
My aunt.	To renovate the walls.
The queen tells you about walls.	Ancient. Solid.
Let her talk.	But worn down by assaults and
She likes to listen to herself.	Eroded by the years.
I really don't have much time.	These walls were built during the first attacks on
I got into the system, but the firewall's going to bite me in the ass.	our city.
	And we have maintained them ever since.
And it's not because I'm the king's daughter that	My father always told us we had to take care of them.

Crap! Shouldn't talk to you
about myself.
It's not important.
I need to talk about Andy.
You need to know.
Fuck!
Andy's dead.
And Henry the hero is dead.
Only one was allowed a
funeral.
A fucking state funeral.
Make believe on an epic
scale.
And the other, we forget.
We erase.
We enthrone him in a cave
and lose the key.
And then we look elsewhere.
Because heroes are the ones
that shout what we want
to hear louder than every-
one else.
That's all.
The real heroes, those who
are brave.
Those who dare, end up
destroyed by the bomb
inside that couldn't survive
our betrayal.
But I have honour.
And yes, yes, I'm not
ashamed to say it, love.

They are our first line of
defence.
My brother did not do it.
He left.
It is my duty to defend us.
Henry defended us.
But men cannot do it all.
We must
I want
To build the walls higher.
I worry about fissures.
Fractures.
Particularly the east wing.
We must reinforce the gates.
We will spare no expense.
Our masons, our engineers,
our blacksmiths will work
round the clock.
They are our heroes.
Those who maintain
the wall.
They are not just assem-
bling brick and metal.
This wall. It is us.
United. Strong. Brave.
Heroic.
It is thanks to them.
Their ancestral know-how.
The new techniques they
have developed
That we will survive.

But that's not why.
That's not why I'm showing
you this.
I'm not some emo teen
widow.
And even less an atten-
tion-starved Juliet.
I always spat on love.
Because it pulls you off
course.
It makes you see everything
in full colour, in rose-tinted
glasses, with little hearts,
and the truth is that I'll
never see life any differ-
ently than I do now.
But Andy.
Andy saw beyond truth.
He had X-ray vision.
He saw right through
me. He saw clear through
everything.
Except himself.
I was the only one who
could do that.
But not always.
Not enough.
I let him down, let him slip
through my fingers.
But now, I hold on tight to
our hearts and I charge.

This wall is their
masterwork.
There are those of you
whose parents are among
these noble workers.
And others who hope to
join their ranks.
I admire their work.
I thank them for their
efforts.
I am constantly amazed at
what we can build.
These majestic towers.
Ramparts
Parapets
Gate mechanisms
Locks
All of this attests to our
ingenuity.
And we must continue
Always
To build them higher.
More walls.
More towers.
This ambitious plan is what
I hold dear.

In ALISON's mic, we hear the sounds of the police in the distance.
She cuts comms.

REGINA
It is remarkable, is it not?
And all of this is to ensure that future generations can ben-
efit from our city's boon.
The future.
What lies ahead.
It concerns you.
Alison.
Princess.
Future queen.
You don't know her yet.
Little Miss Serious.
We kept her in the shadows.
She is
She will be a great queen.
For our city.
I will watch over her.
And over you.
I would have liked to introduce her to you.
But the grief.
You understand.
She and Henry.
Cousins, so close
We had almost hoped
Anyway.

3. THE PRINCESS

Suddenly ALISON *enters, out of breath. She has her bag with her laptop. She takes a bottle of water.*

ALISON
It's hella dark in here.

She looks around, sees the neon H. REGINA *stands up and faces her.*

REGINA
Didn't you hear the edict?

ALISON
Why the circus?

REGINA
I was worried.

ALISON
This is what, a chapel for Henry? What else are you going to conjure?

ALISON *goes to open the curtains.*
REGINA *stands up to draw them closed, but* ALISON *stops her.*

The technician makes a move to intervene; REGINA *waves them off.*

REGINA
You ought to have been at the cemetery this morning. With us.

ALISON
I couldn't.

REGINA
Too busy living the hectic life of a princess?

ALISON
I'm not a princess.

REGINA
But you are. Your father was king.

ALISON
Not anymore.

REGINA
You are still a member of the family. You must always remember that.

ALISON
What family?

REGINA
We used to be close.

ALISON
When I was twelve and had my hair in pigtails.

REGINA
What's changed?

ALISON
I got older.

REGINA
Because you're so old now. And wise to boot.

ALISON *(indicating the neon lights)*
What's all this? Can't be for him.

REGINA
It is for us. Our grief.

ALISON
Because, at his burial, we're what's important. Of course.
Appearances are all you care about.

REGINA
You ought to have been there this morning.

ALISON
For you.

REGINA
For the family.

ALISON
You make it sound like we're the Mafia!

REGINA
I demand to know where you were.

REGINA shuts off her mic then signals to the technician to play music in our headsets. ALISON does not turn off her mic, which enables us to hear the conversation.

ALISON
You're not my mother.

REGINA
I am the leader.

ALISON
I was at the cemetery. Farther in.

REGINA
Why didn't you join us?

ALISON
You weren't at the right grave.

REGINA
Are you saying that we missed the one with the honour guard, flag, photograph and flowers? That wasn't Henry's grave?

ALISON
It wasn't Andy's grave.

REGINA
You'll stop this Andy nonsense!
I have one son and he's called Henry.

ALISON
Henry the valiant.
The fucking knight.
The king of the city!

REGINA
Watch your language.
Henry was a brilliant boy!

ALISON
A real little star.
Or maybe a comet. Whose brilliance flamed out over our heads.
I'm not brilliant.
I live in shadow.
Little Miss Serious.
And it was in the dark that I saw.
Andy appear.
You lie.
You've got more than one son.

REGINA
That's absurd.
You're rewriting history.

ALISON
No, it's the same story.
The same boy.

I know his heart
But you're fixed on his face.
To save yours.

REGINA
No! You will not take that tone with me.
Never.
You will stop being impertinent and playing the wild child.
You will toe the line!
You will do what Henry did.
He would have been a true king.
And now all that this city has left is you.
Be worthy!

ALISON
I'll never be like Henry.
I'll never be like you.
I'll never be queen.
Andy knew it.
He refused to follow you.
He refused to follow your orders.
He disobeyed.
Andy knew.
And that's why he's dead.

REGINA
How dare you?
My son Henry never refused an order.
He was an exemplary soldier.
You dishonour his memory.
This is blasphemy. He died this morning! You've no right!

ALISON
Finally! I thought nothing could shake you anymore.

REGINA
I will not allow you to tarnish his memory!

ALISON
Straight ahead in the cemetery. Straight ahead of us.
All for show.
Like magic.
Then, like in all good magic shows, something disappears.

REGINA
Alison . . .

ALISON
But that's all right. I know where he is.

REGINA
Henry is buried in the cemetery under the flags.

ALISON approaches the technician. She pushes something on the console and shuts off the music. Surprised, the technician does nothing to stop her.

ALISON
Not anymore.

REGINA
What did you do?

ALISON
I reworked your design. It wasn't right.
To make everyone believe that Henry's in the cemetery,
when we both know it's all smoke and mirrors.

REGINA (*to those assembled*)
Silence! Do not listen to her. She is delirious. It is the grief.
A phase.

ALISON
What did Henry die of?

REGINA
That is confidential.

*REGINA **signals to the technician to put the music back on**.*

ALISON
No more make-believe?

REGINA
It is a state secret.

ALISON
Whoa, I'm scared.

REGINA
You should be.
You should shut up and listen.
You should do what we tell you to do.
You have a future. Do not destroy it.

ALISON
"I am your future."

REGINA
Since Henry is gone.
You will succeed him.

ALISON
I'm not "one day." I'm now.

REGINA
Now, you're nothing but a child. You know nothing.
Everything lies before you. Be thankful for that.

ALISON
I don't give a shit about your future. I want the truth, right
now. I want Andy.

REGINA
Calm down. It'll be over soon. We'll go back home. You'll
go back to playing in your room, playing with your toys.
You'll return to school. Everything will be as it was.

ALISON
I won't forget him.

REGINA
Honouring his memory does you honour.

ALISON
That's what I want to do. He was the one who told me. He
was the one who opened my eyes.

REGINA
To what?

ALISON
What's behind the walls.

REGINA
No.

ALISON
Andy told me everything.
Revealed it all.
Since yesterday, I see.
Since yesterday, I'm no longer a child. I'll never be a child again.
Yesterday, the world was wild and magnificent. Today, it's terrible.
Yesterday,
I was playing *Assassin's Creed*. I was flying rooftop to rooftop. I was killing bad guys in my flying suit. Very late.
Too late.
A text.
—Meet me. I have to show you something. Andy.
So I go. Like always. I go to his window. I wait.
—Crap, where are you?
No answer. A stick figure doodled on the wall. Winking at me. An arrow. His tag.
A game. You've got to be fucking kidding me. He made me a game! I look around. I see his tag. I follow him like Thumbelina. I jump, I climb, I fly! Under the stars I'm like the Princess of Persia moving through the grey night of cats and bats. The arrows guide me. I laugh. It's a game.

Our game. I get to the end of the road, the end of the world.
Our city stops at the walls. Like a medieval map, those
who keep going fall off. It's an abyss.
I catch my breath. Nothing. The arrows have disappeared.
No trace of Andy.
I don't text him. I'll find him. No clues. I've got my pride.
Drawn by the emptiness, I approach.
And I see.

Beat.

And I understand why my father plucked out his eyes.

REGINA
You made that up.

ALISON
Why would I do that?

REGINA
Because if you were found on the walls, I would have no
choice but to order your execution.

ALISON
That's intense.

REGINA
That is the law.
Did anyone see you?

ALISON
See me?! That's what's bothering you?

No one saw me on the wall! No one saw me at the cemetery! I'm invisible, see? Just like Andy! I've been erased!

ALISON approaches the console and outmanoeuvres the technician to turn off the music in our headsets.

REGINA
Calm down. Not in front of them.

ALISON
Who cares? You'll just buy them off when they leave.

REGINA *(to those assembled)*
She does not mean that.

ALISON
She says what she means.
You don't know your own son!

REGINA
Neither do you.

ALISON *(suddenly serious)*
I know.
I know everything.
Listen to me.
Regina, you must—

REGINA
Go sit down. Put on your headset.

REGINA receives a call.

She looks at ALISON.

No. I haven't seen her. She hasn't been here. Continue your search. And watch the walls. What? They tried to get in? How many? Where's the army? What are you doing? Get me the general.

ALISON *stands up to leave.* REGINA *stops her with a gesture.*

You stay.
I'll be back.

REGINA *exits.*

4. THE CITY AND THE WALLS

ALISON
I've never been on the Great Wall of China.
I was born too late for the Berlin Wall.
The world carries on and keeps building them.
Everywhere.
Between Austria and Slovenia.
Between Slovenia and Croatia.
Between Croatia and Hungary.
Between Hungary and Serbia.
Between Mexico and the United States.
Between Ukraine and Russia.
Between Russia and Estonia.
Between Bulgaria and Turkey.
Between Turkey and Greece.

Beat.

I don't know.
I don't know what the brick thinks.
I don't know what the brick thrown against a wall thinks.
A wall of bricks.
Does the wall collapse?

Does the brick explode?
Do the bricks ask what's happening to them?
A bunch of bricks stacked together is a wall.
A single brick is a weapon.
Andy made me watch kung fu videos.
Where the guy breaks rocks with his bare hands.
We thought it was super cool.
We preferred to write on the walls.
Not very prince- and princess-like
But it was our way to reach out to those we could reach.
All of you.
Without it sounding fake.
Contrived.
Plus it was our secret.
This is our city, after all!
Henry said we were the masters of our own destiny.
Nothing's written.
We're just chaos on the move.
We're the ones who make sense of it.
Of life.
So, to prove it, he decided
To change his name.
To stop being Henry
It was his father's name, and his grandfather's before him.
And all those kings.
A name and a number.
That wasn't him.
He wasn't another Henry in a line of Henrys.
He was himself.
Henry became Andy.
Overnight.

She approaches the neon H. She moves the two neon bars to their furthest points, transforming the H into an A. The technician watches her. They don't know what to do. ALISON moves towards them and hands over a USB key, which they take. She heads back towards us.

We were like Batman, and Bruce Wayne.
I was ALIe.
Like the boxer. Ali.
The best boxer in the world.
And Ali
Because he stuck to his ideals.
Even though they stripped him of his title.
Andy's tag was like an anarchist A.
Good God, his mother would've lost it.
And we'd leave our marks like a game.
To follow
To be found.
It was just a game.
We were just kids.
We didn't know anything.

Beat.

Fuck you, Andy! Fuck you and your fucking treasure hunt.
Fuck you and your little boy pain.
Because that's what you are: a little boy in major pain.
The immense suffering of a child in the body of a man not built to take it.
You're taking on water, Andy.
You're drowning in yourself.
It's leaking all over the place.

Splashing over me.
Your pain's coming down on everyone.
On me, on the walls, on—
My memory's full of you.
Of moments stolen by your pain.
I've stocked them all up, I run them in a loop
To figure out
To find a clue
Were you sad when you were with me?
Were you sad when you loved me?
Because you knew
At every step.
You knew every step was bringing you closer to the end.
You always told me you were afraid of fate.
That it wasn't fate who decided.
That you were free.
Then you decided you were free of it.
At every clue on every wall.
You knew
That you wanted to lead me to your loss.
My loss of you.
I don't accept that, Andy.
I can't accept that you're lost.
That you're somewhere I'm not.
That your pain has won.
That the waves living inside you broke on the rocks.
That you're lost for nothing. All alone. Without me.
Fuck you and your game.
Fuck you and your fate.
Fuck! Fuck! Fuck!
I can only see his body.
Not Andy.

Just a corpse. Devoid of him.
On the rocks at the foot of the wall.
And there was the sun.
The shadow grew.
Like a drop of oil of the ground.
As though his soul was slipping away.
And my eye followed it.
And my gaze stretched.
And I understood.
That Andy's corpse was not the treasure.
But the last tag. The last sign. The last arrow.
Andy's corpse was a pagan compass.
Pointing towards the ghosts.
A village of white tents that had appeared overnight.
That the curtain of darkness had revealed as it was drawn.
These children, these women, these men. Alive.
Invisible.
I saw them approach.
Follow the shadow in reverse.
Approach the rocks.
Recognize the corpse as Andy.
A young god who fell from the sky too soon.
Carry him away.
In silence.
In a dignified procession.

REGINA has entered without ALISON noticing.

REGINA
You lie.

ALISON
I'm saying what I saw.

REGINA
You can't. You can't do that! You can't come in here and do
whatever you want!

REGINA restores the neon H.

It's like you want to destroy all our dignity.

ALISON
There is no dignity in a lie.
I want the truth.
Not like this morning.

REGINA
I saw a burial this morning.
We all saw a burial this morning.
You want me to replay the video for you?

ALISON
What about me!
Me.
What about what I saw?
I turned back, towards the city.
The morning had barely begun.
The day had not yet come.
But you had.
On the city walls.

I saw you.
Panicked.
No more Henry!

REGINA
No.

ALISON
On the surveillance cameras.
Upon waking. Your guards told you.
They woke you up to tell you.
So you came to confirm Andy's death!

REGINA
There was nothing on the walls.

ALISON
No one.
You washed the rocks!
His blood disappeared.
And Henry died a glorious death.
How convenient for everyone!
Fuck. Fuck. Fuck!
It explains everything.
You chose your city over your son!

REGINA
No!
It's not.
I can't.
I can't accept Henry's death.
Do you understand?

I can't accept that my flesh and blood is dead.
A piece of myself torn away
My heart's in tatters
My son surrendered to death, do you know what
that's like?
Do you know what it's like to have questions no one can
answer?
Do you know what it's like when the world trembles?
When the order of life is upset?
When sense stops and the head spins?
Yes, I understood why your father plucked out his eyes.
Why he left.
Why he left it all behind.
When tragedy struck.
Shedding light on this brutal world.
The nausea that rises
The sea that smashes against the rocks.
I breathe
I breathe
How can I still be here and he elsewhere?
I cried out on the walls.
Then I smothered my cries.
And my tears.
And I turned back to the city.
For whom I am also mother.
I could not leave it.
This child could not be abandoned a second time.
Our family could not do that to it again.
Alone, one is at leisure to wallow in shame and pain.
I do not have that luxury.
I must stay.
I don't even have a place to see my son's body.

He floats at sea.
And I refuse to wake up every morning
To look at the sea and remember that it's a vast grave.
No.
I'd go mad.
For real.
So, I imagined what should have been.
Since the world decided differently
I refuse.
I want my son.
Henry was born to be a hero and this city's pride.
So he will be.
In spite of the gods and fate.
We will remember my son as a hero who enabled the city
to endure.
Like all of our family.
And you, too.
I designed
The funeral I would have wanted for him.
What a mother never wants.
A queen must.
You didn't see a thing.
Look:
In the full light of day.
Before the whole city.
His body is framed by white satin.
The scent of irises
And the product they use for embalming
Overpowers.
It's cold.
My little man is cold.
My son sleeps in his uniform.

Tired from too much studying.
Too much work.
My son with his medals.
My proud son.
Henry.
I take him in my arms.
I remove his ring.
I shut the casket.
I place a photograph of him in his uniform.
The men from the garrison arrive.
They carry his casket.
Military music plays.
At the cemetery,
I stand tall in my black dress
I'm cold.
It feels like it comes from within.
As though a cold black hole's appeared in my gut.
Breathe
Breathe
A queen never panics.
And I never burn out.
I am a beacon.
I am a beacon.
I rise
I throw earth into the hole.
His soul is underground.
Everything is in order.
Henry's soul is at peace.

ALISON
Not Andy's.

REGINA
You're the only one who calls him that.
I wrote his name on the stone.
Henry.
For all eternity.
Forget Andy.

ALISON
I can't.
He gave me his memory to treasure.

REGINA
What?

ALISON
I followed them.
It was cold.
We had nothing.
In a camp
Of misfortune.
Filled with patchwork lives
Everyone lending what they didn't have.
They managed to find,
For this dead stranger,
Everything to honour his dignity.
To recall his humanity
And ours.
Scarred women wept for your son.
Starved men washed your son.
As the solemn children watched.
They wrapped him in three pieces of white cloth.
They prayed.

They sang a heart-rending song.
They adopted him among their dead.
Your son's buried on the right side.
Without a casket.
His head faces Mecca.

REGINA
That's impossible.

ALISON
I wept with them.
I thanked them.
I played guitar.
We stood in silent prayer.
I, who never prays, I prayed with them.
Faced with death, everything becomes sacred.
They gave me back his phone.

REGINA
Henry is a hero.

ALISON
Andy is a hero.
He gave me the gift of truth.

REGINA
He wanted to defend the city.

ALISON
Shut your mouth!

REGINA
Alison!

ALISON
You're the one burying yourself in lies.
I received the alert.
On Andy's phone.
Citizens,
We must take refuge
Immediately
In the heart of the city
For our own safety.
The lone threat does not exist.
Those who buried your son are dying outside the city!

REGINA
Andy is not my son.

ALISON
I'll show all of it to everyone.
I filmed it all on his cell.
Look!

REGINA advances calmly. She takes the cell.
She holds it gently, a memento.
She watches a video we can't see but that we can hear.
Refugees.
REGINA stops the video.
REGINA looks outside.
Suddenly, REGINA takes the phone and destroys it with one smack against the table.
She hits it very hard.

She loses control.
A breakdown.
Taken aback, ALISON watches her.

REGINA
There's nothing outside this city but a storm, do you
hear me?
Leave.

ALISON
Regina . . .

REGINA
Go home. Throw out your clothes. Burn them. You'll play
your video games, and you'll not leave the house until I call
you. No backtalk. Let me handle this.

ALISON
But everyone here saw.

REGINA
What did they see, exactly?
Nothing.
A broken phone.
Put your headsets on. Forget the girl. Forget the story.
Because that is all it is. Lies. Since her father left. She is
nothing but trouble. She spends all her time cooped up
in her room. Like now. She is not here. Put your headsets
back on. Put on the music!

ALISON doesn't move.

I'm doing this for you!

ALISON
No, you're not. You're throwing me a lifeline to save yourself. That's not the same thing. For the family.

REGINA
What do you think you'll gain by this? There's nothing left. Henry will not come back. No one will commend you.

ALISON
We don't all toil for glory.

REGINA
Alison, you're an intelligent young lady. You have a future. I can help you. You've a chance to have the life you want. Wait. Think. Go home. Sleep. Play music. Watch TV. Go dancing. Meet another boy. Live. Choose life.

ALISON
I don't care about any of that.

REGINA
Stubborn as a mule! Just like your father. Arrogant!

ALISON
It runs in the family.

REGINA
You're not a heroine! You're nothing but a clueless child.

ALISON

I'm so much more powerful than you. I'm not afraid of
anyone. You'd throw me to the guards even if it grates on
your soul. Is that what you call being the boss of everything? You're just a stupid bureaucrat. A fucking slave!

REGINA

I'm giving you one more chance.

ALISON

You shouldn't gamble. Your poker face is terrible.

REGINA

Alison . . .

ALISON

I'm not the little annoyance you think I am. I'm not doing
this to be a pain in your ass. It's so much more than that.
I'm not doing it because it's what Andy wanted. It's not
about some little crush. I'm doing it because it's the decent,
humane thing to do.
I know the truth; I don't need your endorsement!
I'm free
It's my life!
Float like a butterfly! Sting like a bee!
Float like a butterfly! Sting like a bee!
And you can destroy all the phones you want!
I've uploaded it all online.

*REGINA grabs ALISON by the arm and escorts her out of the
classroom.*

5. DESTRUCTION

They are outside the room.

REGINA *(furious)*
You've destroyed everything! Everything!
There's no turning back.

The technician raises the volume in our headsets. We hear their conversation.

There's nothing more I can do!
Don't you understand?!
What can I say?
What can I do for it to penetrate and stay in your head?
You're going to die, Alison!
You're going to make me say
You're going to make me do
You've made me sign your death warrant.
Why do this to me?
After all I've done.
We
All we are.
You're the future
You were
Our dynasty.

This is no longer a game. It's real life.
I'm going to
You're going to
No, it's impossible
Not you too
I don't want
Too many deaths
Why do you summon death to the city?
Why don't you ever choose life?
You seek out chaos
You want to destroy us.
You make me out to be a monster.
A heartless harpy
Look at me
I don't recognize myself anymore
You're the guilty one but I'm the one accused.
You've wanted to destroy the city since the beginning
I won't let you
I won't let you
I'll live to be a hundred
And I'll return
Again
But I won't let you destroy our city.

ALISON
I don't want to destroy the city. And I don't want to die.
You've given me no choice.

REGINA
We will stand united. Every brick. Together.

ALISON
I want to talk to you. You say that I can't reason. And yet. I want a dialogue.

REGINA
We will remain, our roots planted in our soil.

ALISON
Outside, people are dying.

REGINA
There are people. Our people. Dying inside. The refugees don't have a monopoly on disease, hunger and fear.

ALISON
We've got to let them in.

REGINA
And put them where? We don't have enough space for our own sick. What do we feed them? With what money? And our poor, where do we put them?

ALISON
We've got space. Everywhere. We can put them here. We can put them in the palace!

REGINA
You want to put people we don't know in the palace. Among them thieves, criminals, terrorists. In our homes, our rooms, our museums, our palaces? You want to admit the starving foxes to our henhouse and hope nothing goes wrong?

ALISON
They aren't criminals, or foxes. They're people. Children.
Families.

REGINA
Are you ready to die for people you don't know?

ALISON
Between the interests of the state and values, I choose
values every time!

ALISON enters and addresses the audience.

There's something greater, right?
Life's not just rules, right?
Isn't there something more fundamental?
I thought
I thought you'd understand.
Because, yes, before being the inhabitants of a city.
A line traced on the ground.
Before drawing a line. An imaginary line.
A little dividing line between us
We're all the same species
On the same planet.
A country is imagined
A people is imagined
How much time does it take to become a people?
Truly?
One year?
A hundred?
Three thousand?
Ten minutes?

Are they any less our sisters and brothers because they
come from the other side of a line?
Really?

And they die.
Every second.
They gasp for breath.
The heart stops.
A child.
While you won't listen.
Another.
While you refuse to hear.
Their mother.
While you stay seated.
Their father.
A family has died.
It won't stop.
While we talk.
Right beside us.
Isn't that more important than the municipal deficit?

REGINA
Yes.
Empires have died.
For leaving their gates open.
And for not being vigilant about who entered.
Think of Rome.
We will not fall.
The walls are solid.
And will remain closed.

ALISON

I don't want to win for myself. I want justice!
I want everyone to know the truth.

REGINA

What will the truth tell you? That we're monsters? That
we don't want to help others? That we're at fault? Of
course we're all at fault. We're all scared. We all want to
stay alive. Survival, that's the truth. The city's survival.
You knew what you were doing. You didn't do it for us. You
did it for yourself.

ALISON

I answer to a higher power. Dying for this doesn't faze me.
Because there have to be values that we're willing to die
for. A line where we say, that, that's enough, no further.
And to have the courage to hold the line. Like on the soccer
field. I don't want anything else. I hold my line. If I die for
it, so be it. I'll have held it. And the whole city will know.
It will know that I've got principles. And it will rise up. To
hold my line.

REGINA

The city will never follow you.

ALISON

We shall see.

REGINA

If you incite them to follow you in this madness
I'll have to protect them from themselves.
And I will give the order to open fire

On them and on all those who stand with them.
We're at war, don't you understand?
We're under siege.
I still wear the crown here!
But you, you prefer to die for them rather than carry on
our dynasty?
If only
If only
All of this could've been avoided.
But you had to have principles.

ALISON
I'll tell them everything.
I'll talk to them.
They'll understand.
It's about human dignity
Nothing more.
The citizens will agree to welcome the refugees.

REGINA
Alison

ALISON
Death will not gorge today.
Open the gates!

REGINA
Never.

ALISON
I accept.

REGINA
What?

ALISON
I accept the crown.

REGINA
You don't have a choice.

ALISON
No, I accept the dynasty. I accept all of it.
I will be the little princess.
I will be the girl you always wanted
I will be even more brilliant than Henry.
I will be the one who stands straight and true.

REGINA
Alison . . .

ALISON
But then I want the crown right away.
I will be queen.
And I'll let everyone enter.
And the city will be full.
You won't be able to do anything!
One day
One day
You say I am your future.
And yet
You know very well that's what I'll do!
And you know that I'm right to do it!
You don't have a choice!

REGINA
Yes.

ALISON
Who will you save?

Beat.

REGINA
I sentence you.
To exile.

ALISON
No!

REGINA
You will be escorted to the gates.

ALISON
Regina!

REGINA
You are no longer one of us.

ALISON
You can't.

REGINA
You no longer belong to us.

ALISON
I am yours! We have the same blood. You can't.

REGINA
This betrayal will destroy you. You are no longer mine. I do not want you. Leave.

ALISON
I won't be erased.

REGINA
You no longer have the right to speak. You are no longer one of us. You are no longer anyone.

ALISON
So I'll join them.

She quickly exits.

REGINA calls security on her Bluetooth device.

REGINA
She just came by here. I saw her outside.

6. PURSUIT

The technician signals for us to put on our headsets. Police comms are transmitted through the headsets.

UNIT 5
Police! Stop!

UNIT 8
Drop your weapon! Now!
On the ground! On the ground!

UNIT 5
She's getting something out of her jacket!

UNIT 8
Watch out!

UNIT 8 fires.

UNIT 5
No! What have you done?

UNIT 8
She was . . . she was . . .

UNIT 3
Unit 5, situation report.

UNIT 5
She's on the ground. Unit 3, call an ambulance.

UNIT 8
A cellphone! She was a holding a cellphone!

UNIT 5
Shit!

UNIT 8
Shit! Shit! Shit!

UNIT 5
Calm down.

Rumbling. The thunder has arrived. And the migrants are entering the city.

UNIT 3
Emergency at the east gate! They are coming in! I repeat, the migrants are coming in. In the thousands. We are over-run. We need reinforcements! Attention, all units. Get to the east gate on the double!

UNIT 8
We can't leave her! I'll stay. We're still waiting for the ambulance.

We hear a crowd, shots, helicopters, chaos.

UNIT 3
The ambulances are stuck, the streets are blocked. They won't make it. Get over here on the double! We can't hold them off much longer!

UNIT 8
Wait. We can still save her.

UNIT 5
Stop! She's not breathing.

UNIT 3
What the hell are you doing, dammit? We need everyone here! They're coming in like rats!

UNIT 5
Let's take care of the living. We'll see to the dead later.

UNIT 8
I'll be right there.

UNIT 5
But . . .

UNIT 8
I'll be right there.

UNIT 5 exits, leaving UNIT 8 alone with ALISON's body. We hear helicopters over the city. In our headsets, we can still hear UNIT 8.

Our children die before us.
First Prince Henry.

Then Princess Alison.
We are damned.
The gods are against us.
This city will not last.
All will collapse.
The walls cannot stand.
Alison, what did you want to tell me,
To show me on your phone?
What is this?
What did you record?

ALISON's video, made by Andy. We hear her.

ALISON
"Really? No. Don't film me. Andy, come on. Okay. Okay.
I thought about the idea you had yesterday.
And we can't leave.
We can't leave all this.
We're in line.
And even if we weren't.
It's our duty to stay.
I won't be like my father.
I'll never leave, despite the horror.
We have to stay and fight.
Like Ali.
That's courage.
Regina's right.
Even if
Regina's wrong.
Also.
Because we've got to stay and change things
Andy

For us
For everyone.
We're the future.
We're now.
We can do it all, Andy.
Don't be sad.
We are who we are.
We're strong.
We'll change the world, Andy.
We will change the fucking world.
It will be beautiful.
It will become our world.
Just the way we want.
I don't really know what that is.
But we'll figure it out.
It will be a lot of work.
But before all that.
I'll kick your ass at *Prince of Persia*
Then we'll make like cats on the rooftops.
See the sun rise over the city.
The walls will be ours.
We'll leave our tags everywhere.
Like a refrain.
The whole city will sing.
So our memories remain.
And so they'll recall
That things can change."

Fin

ACKNOWLEDGEMENTS

MCV: I would like to thank Alexis Diamond for her perceptive and kind gaze on my work and for her friendship, and Annie Gibson and her team at Playwrights Canada Press. I also wish to thank the Canada Council for the Arts and the Conseil des arts et des lettres du Québec for their support in the development of the original work.

AD: I would like to thank Marie-Claude Verdier for her faith and her friendship, and Annie Gibson and her team at Playwrights Canada Press, Blake Sproule and Jessica Lewis, for their support and investment in our work. I would also like to acknowledge the contribution of mentor and teacher Frank Heibert and the participants of Playwrights' Workshop Montréal's 2019 Exploring Practice—Theatre Translation intensive, where I first presented a very rough excerpt of the first two scenes of *Andy's Gone*. Lastly, thanks to Lynn Kozak (McGill University) for sharing her literal translation of the Sophocles text.

MCV + AD: We would also like to thank Jack Paterson of Bouche Theatre Collective for producing and dramaturging a pan-Canadian isolation workshop in the spring of 2020, featuring actors Jenna Thorne and Sabrina Vellani, which contributed to the development of the English translation.

Marie-Claude Verdier's first play, *Je n'y suis plus*, was produced at the National Arts Centre's French Theatre. Her play *Nous autres antipodes* received an honourable mention for the Prix Gratien-Gélinas from the Centre des auteurs/autrices dramatiques (CEAD). In 2018, Marie-Claude became the first playwright-in-residence at the Bibliothèque et Archives nationales du Québec (BAnQ), where she worked on her play *Apparitions*. She is currently working on a sci-fi play, *Seeker*, which Alexis Diamond has been commissioned to translate for Bouche Theatre Collective. Marie-Claude is also a dramaturg and has worked with many distinguished directors, including Marc Beaupré, Christian Lapointe and Benoît Vermeulen. She lives in Laval.

Alexis Diamond is a theatre artist, opera and musical librettist, translator and theatre curator working on both sides of Montreal's linguistic divide. Her award-winning works have been presented across Canada, the US and Europe. In 2018, Alexis began a collaboration with Erin Hurley (McGill University) and Emma Tibaldo (Playwrights' Workshop Montréal) researching the history of English-language theatre in Québec. In May 2019, Alexis served as the co-artistic director of the famed Festival du Jamais Lu, where she presented the mostly French-language *Faux-amis* with co-author Hubert Lemire. Upcoming tours of her theatre translations include *The Problem with Pink* by Érika Tremblay-Roy and Pascal Brullemans's *The Nonexistent*. She lives in Montreal.